MY

BROKEN HEART

SINGS

The Poetry of

Gary A. Burlingame

Healthy Life Press

Published by: Healthy Life Press
Arvada, Colorado 80003
Web site:
www.healthylifepress.com

Cover photos and inside digital photo artwork
by Gary A. Burlingame

Burlingame, Gary A. (1958 -)
My Broken Heart Sings

ISBN 978-0982580073

1. Poetry
2. Inspirational & Religious Poetry

Second edition, 2017
Printed in the United States of America

Praise for My Broken Heart Sings:

Danish philosopher Soren Kierkegaard wrote, "A poet is an unhappy being whose heart is torn by secret sufferings, but whose lips are so strangely formed that when the sighs and the cries escape them, they sound like beautiful music...."

Gary A. Burlingame is one such being, with this difference – once unhappy, due to the loss of a son, his broken heart now sings, because he kept walking by faith. His readers are the beneficiaries of the work of the One who binds up the brokenhearted, "...bestowing on them a crown of beauty instead of ashes, the oil of gladness instead of mourning, and a garment of praise instead of a spirit of despair. They will be called oaks of righteousness, a planting of the LORD for the display of his splendor" (Isaiah 61:1-3).

Gary describes this metamorphosis, "In the days of my youth the songs of my heart were self-focused. My poetry had no clear voice or purpose (outside of wooing my wife). Over time the Lord brought me through some heart-changing experiences. He allowed my heart to break so that He could mold my heart into something new. Out of this regenerated state my poetry grew - expressing what other people could not express - crying out for them. My prayer is that my poetry would give broken hearts an outlet of release. My Broken Heart Sings is a compilation of poems that speak of pain and joy, love and loss, suffering and new birth."

–David B. Biebel, DMin

To my brothers and sisters of faith, Debbie, Dave and Annette, David, Tim and Kathy, and Judy who helped me experience the beauty of grieving together

ACKNOWLEDGEMENTS

First and foremost, I acknowledge our Lord and Savior Jesus Christ; any gift that I have worthy of sharing comes from Him. I acknowledge the Holy Spirit who is responsible for any healing or encouragement that would come out of this work of poetry.

My son Christopher John Burlingame, my friend's son David Anthony Trumbore and, above all, God's son Jesus Christ have had an everlasting impact upon my life's work as evidenced here in this collection of poems.

Without the love and support of my wife Debbie and my daughters, Laura and Corey, I could never have completed this work.

I acknowledge David and Annette Trumbore, who allowed me to enter into their lives and share its hard experiences. It was often through our conversations that I was inspired to express in poetry what our hearts were feeling.

I acknowledge Joe McArdle who put some of my writings to contemporary music. Our music CD, Tear it Down, gave me great encouragement to write more for the Lord. The following poems were included in the music CD: Two Sons, Rescue Me, Your Tears Are So Many, and Psalms for Suffering Hearts.

I acknowledge Ramona Neidig for her technical guidance and encouragement and David B. Biebel for his years of support to finally get my collection of poems into print.

PSALM 42:1-5

PSALM 51:15-17

MATTHEW 11:28-30

2 CORINTHIANS 1:3-4

2 CORINTHIANS 4:16-18

REVELATION 21:1-4

CONTENTS

Preface

Preface

In this compilation of my poems I declare that we have great freedom, through God's grace, to expose our hearts not only in the joy and hope that resides there because of the work of Jesus Christ, but also in great perplexity over intense frustration of living in this fallen world, with the feelings of pain and grief that bear down on us from time to time. We too easily neglect to open our hearts in honest expression. As a result, we withhold our broken hearts from Christ and from each other.

I say, let our hearts break, but not in solitude. Let our hearts be opened in the friendship of a brother or sister (as appropriate) so that Christ may enter in and do a supernatural work that moves us into a better balance between the reality of our sufferings and the true hope and joy of His merciful grace. In Christ, we have such freedom!

MY
BROKEN HEART
SINGS

The Poetry of

Gary A. Burlingame

A Truer World

A friend asked me why I hadn't written about the loss of my own son, Christopher John. It was hard to focus on any particular feeling or to capture everything I needed to say in a single poem. This poem came to me as I prepared for an Easter sunrise service. Without my son I would not have known A Truer World. His death at only six months of age caused me to wrestle with God's Word and sovereignty in order to find our true source of hope and joy.

On a cold December day,
Colder than I've ever known,
I carried you away-
Away from your earthly home-
And I laid you to rest
On that cold December day.
Such a cold December day!

On a cold December day,
Everything just turned around.
My dreams were swept away;
Away from me raising you

Into you changing me-
On that cold December day.
Such a cold December day!

When I needed it most in life
I declared it.
All I ever really had
Came forth in boldness:

Where O death is your sting?
Where O death, your victory?
The sting of death is sin.

And we
Had the victory
Through Christ
On that cold December day.

On a cold December day-
You died a boy and not a man
And I sent you away,
Away from my loving hands
As I laid you to rest
On that cold December day.
Such a cold December day!

Was it the Son who changed the Father?
Do we really know how it should be?
I thought I would be raising you,
But it's you who is changing me.

It was you, my son, who changed my life;
You brought a truer world to me.

As helpless as you were,
You brought a truer world to me.

Why?

Suicide is devastating. The ripple effects are extensive. Not only is precious life lost, but those left behind may never get the answers to the questions that haunt them.

Lord,
I'm sleepwalking
A nightmare.

Don't wake me!
Guide me safely.
Whisper in my ear,
>"I shall not lose
>Even one of you"
So I don't fall away.
Oh I could fall away so easily.

Why
Couldn't I see
Into his eyes
The reason for the tears
He could not cry,
The struggles that waged

So deep inside
Clouding his mind?

Why
Couldn't he
Come home to me
And receive my love
Unconditionally?
Yet another choice
Lie deep inside,
Clouding his mind.

When
Did he decide?

Where
Did this come from?

How
Arose such inner turmoil?

Why
Did he hold in the pain?

Why, why, why?

Should I have
Understood?
I don't think I
Could
If I
Dared to
Ever try.

Why, why, why?

It's more
Than just a question,
It's a slow death
To those
Who survive.

Two Sons

In Two Sons, I share a story about a friend who lost his first-born son. A few years later his wife gave birth to a healthy baby boy. The reality of his two sons, one on earth and one in heaven, deeply touched my heart.

Once my world was happy as a heart beat
And the bliss governed all that I knew.
When a heart beat goes on as immortal,
It will pace all that seems eternal,
Such as joy.

Then my world got trapped in a silence
Where heart beats pounded out my pain.
And I lived as in isolation,
For no one could hear what was missing,
Not in their joy.

Now my world has a fresh new heart beat.
But am I to ignore the silence?
A shadow on all my happiness–
There will always be some fear of pain
In my joy.

Never take me back, Lord– I don't want to go
Where a heart beat leaves the body for a soul

That I can't see,

That I can't hear,

That I can't hold.

Your Tears Are so Many

I don't want to go through
What you had to go through.
Can I even think it
Without trying to hurt you?

Can you try and teach me
How to bear it with you?
Can you even reach me?
I'm not sure you want to.

> Your tears are so many,
> And I can't feel them;
> I can't feel your pain.

> Your tears are so many,
> And I can't heal them;
> I can't heal your pain.

Guess I'll just be silent–
Show you that I love you,
Listen for your crying.....

> I'll cry if I have to!

Lifeline

The hospital nurses were our connection to our son when he was in the hospital. Since he passed away, we now rely on the Lord to be our connection to our son.

> Nurse,
> I was hoping you were on tonight.
> I'm glad you're there.
>
> How's he doing?
>
> Will this be a good day?
>
> Tell him I love him.
>
> Give him a kiss for me.
>
> Is he flushed or is he pale?
>
> I'll send something in the mail.
>
> Please call me if things change
> And stay as my connection-
> My lifeline to my son.

(When the cord was cut
He was taken from me,
And it rips at my heart
That he responds
To you,
And that you know him
Better than I do.)

-----♥-----

Lord,
I was hoping You were on tonight.
I'm glad You're there.

I miss him.

This was not a good day.

Tell him I love him.

I'm glad I have a photograph
To make the memories last.

Please hold him for me until things change.
And stay as my connection-
My lifeline to my son.

In the Night

We can help each other get through hard times, to a limit. Beyond a point it's all in God's hands. At least this is the way I felt when I brought a friend home to spend the night alone because someone she loved had died.

Once again around the block.
One more time, one last stop,
And one more prayer as the night rolled in.

I pulled up to the curb.
We sat, not saying a word
Because we knew this night would come.

> Lord,
> Her life's turned upside down
> And how quickly she could drown:
> She had no chance to say goodbye.

Into the night I drove away.
I turned to look, saw her wave-
Taking her time to close the door.

We did everything
To stay preoccupied.

From morning
Past noon,
But the hour
Came too soon-
And the night rolled in.

     When memories stir up feelings all too fresh,
     And our souls get to reeling in loneliness,
     This is where You come in, Lord.

We did everything
To stay preoccupied.
We laughed.
We talked.
We ate.
We walked,
Until the night rolled in.

I pulled out from the curb
With my trust in You, Lord,
Because You knew this night would come.

     In the shadows,
        In the silence,
           In the night.

     That is where You come in, Lord!

Psalms for Suffering Hearts

The book of Psalms is filled with rejoicing and it is also filled with expressions of sorrow and grief. I find comfort in knowing that such expressions exist in God's Word, because they exist in my life. However, whether rejoicing or suffering, we need to always remember where lasting peace is found– in the assurance of our salvation!

I call to You Lord, every day;
O my strength, come quickly to me.
Listen to my cry for mercy-
Is Your love declared in the grave?
Be merciful for I am faint
And my bones they grow very weak.
My eyes, they grow weak with sorrow.
My soul and body grow weak with grief.

Oh, be not far from me, O my God;
I'm a deaf man who cannot hear.
The light has gone from my eyes.
O Lord, how fleeting is my life?

All night, in my bed, I'm weeping
For my pain is forever with me.
I call out as my heart grows faint–
Why, O Lord, do You hide Your face?

I wait for You, O Lord, and I wait;
Day and night I cry out to You.
When I call, answer me quickly,
Turn your ear, Lord, to hear my cry.
My heart has melted away in me.
The darkness is my closest friend,
And my days they vanish like smoke
As I am reduced to skin and bones.

And I cry, "How long, O Lord, how long?"
My heart is withering like the grass.
I cry out to You to hear me–
Has unfailing love gone forever?

I trust in You, O Lord.

I say, "You are my God."
O Lord, save me.
O Lord, save me.
Answer me quickly before my spirit fails.

O Lord, save me.
O Lord, save me.
As my life draws near to the grave.

Yet my peace
Comes from my assurance:

Born on faith,

Given by grace,

When I wait–

Wait on You.

The Gospel of Grief

I experience grief through the loss of people I love. I have prayed that God would give me a similar sense of grief and compassion for people who do not know Jesus Christ; for those who are spiritually dead while yet physically alive.

(Ecclesiastes 12)

(I've learned to cry over those who die
And for those in grief who are left behind.
Lord, help me to grieve over those I love
Who are dead to you while still alive.)

Oh, remember your Lord, your God
Before the sun and stars grow dark;
When the strongest men stoop
And their arms shake with age–
When housekeepers tremble.

Oh, remember the Lord, your God,
Before your grinders cease,
Your sight is almost gone;
Your ears no longer hear–
And doors to the street are closed.

Remember your Creator
When you rise up to the birds
Because you can't sleep at night;
Before all songs grow faint,
Before your hair turns gray.

Remember Him
Before the silver cord is severed.

Remember Him
Before mourners go to the streets.

Remember Him
Since your spirit needs a place to go.

Remember your Creator
In the days of your youth
While you are still alive,
Before you have to say
"My days have no value."

In the Balance

In facing the reality of our brokenness, God's supernatural grace and love give us a hope and a joy that is hard to explain. It is often in times of pain and suffering that we feel closest to, and most focused on our Lord.

Lord,
There's something strange in suffering
That the world can't understand:
When life's distractions fade like ghosts,
When reality draws me close
To You.

For only You can make
Joy and pain come out
In the balance.

Only You can make
Joy and pain co-exist
In the balance.

In the balance I give up.
In the balance You restore.

In the balance pain can speak.
　　In the balance hearts can weep.

In the balance You control.
　　In the balance You draw close.

In the balance faith holds fast–
　　And joy will last.

From the hands that held all pain
It's amazing how love flows:
Your love it sets the limit
Beyond which I cannot go,
And You are in control
　　Of the balance.

In the balance hangs my pain.
　　In the balance swings my joy.

In the balance lies escape
　　In the balance held by grace,

In the balance, not by works.
　　In the balance of Your love.

In the balance I can see
　　Hope for me.

Do Your Hands Still Hurt?

This is dedicated to those who live with chronic physical trauma and pain; who have had their lives permanently changed and who feel they have no one to talk to because no one could possibly understand what they are going through.

Friend to Sufferer:

> Just a snap of God's fingers
> Keeps me from being you–
> A thin transparent film
> Hangs between us.
> I know it seems to you
> Like I'm in the best of health.
> Yet if I said that God,
> Our sovereign God,
> Holds me where I am-
> That you face reality
> More than me-
> It doesn't help you out.
> You're on your back,
> I'm standing up,
> While the same God holds us both.

Intercessory Prayer:

Lord, cover him with grace
Like oil upon his bones.
Just a portion of Your grace
A long way will go.
Lord, cover him with grace;
For You are the end
To endless pain.

Sufferer's Plea:

Oh, the aches of my body:
Come now, Lord, I think,
For my soul is consumed
And there's no rest.
Whether I sit or stand,
Even if I sleep, I still ache.
Have mercy on me, Lord,
There's no escape:
It takes everything
Down to the marrow of my life–
To my bone.
Yet if I plead three times
"Take it from me,"
You'll likely say
"My grace is sufficient."

All I want to know,
Lord Jesus–
All I want to know:
Do Your hands still hurt
From being nailed to the cross?
Do Your hands still hurt?

If Your hands still hurt
Then maybe there's hope
That I can be healed.
If Your hands still hurt
Then maybe there's hope
New faith will reveal
Your all sufficient grace.
Do Your hands still hurt?

Intercessory Prayer:

Lord, cover him with grace:
Let him see Your hands.
So bone doesn't grind on bone,
Lord, let him see Your face.
Just a portion of Your grace
A long way will go,
For You are the end
To endless pain.

Breath of Life

This poem was written for Libby, a friend who had emphysema. Her daily struggle to breathe reminded me that every breath I take is precious and worthy for praising God – our Breath of Life.

O Lord of lords,
You formed us from the dust of the ground.
Into our nostrils You breathed
The breath of life.

How I wait on You
For every breath that I take.
It's by Your grace I can breathe–
O Breath of Life.

I breathe out
Never knowing I'll ever breathe back in.
You sustain me breath by breath,
O Breath of Life.

Every breath that I take
Must come from You–
On You I depend
For breath of life.

O Breath of Life,
I'm weak in strength,
What shall I do?

O Breath of Life,
Yet without fear
Of losing You.

     Breath by breath
Draw me closer–
     Breath by breath, Lord,
To Your side.
     Breath by breath,
I will praise You-
     Breath by breath, each
Breath of mine.
     Breath by breath,
Without strength–

Just breath by breath.

      Breath by breath-
 Even dry bones
      Breath by breath, Lord,
Come alive.
      Breath by breath,
When You give them
      Breath by breath, Lord,
Breath of life.
      Breath by breath
I live for You, Lord–
      Breath by breath.

Rescue Me

Suffering can be so overwhelming that we find ourselves stripped of all reason and strength and faith. On the other hand, intense honesty over our helplessness can result in a deeper relationship with our Lord and Shepherd, Jesus Christ. This poem came out of telephone conversations with a close friend who had lost his first-born son. As I entered into his pain, I found these words to express his suffering.

(Dear Lord, I love You so,
And I don't want to let You go.
But it's a circle any more and I just don't know.
My faith is failing and I just don't know.)

I know what David cried, I do–
I even cried the whole night through.
But You go on watching me;
What do You see?

If this goes on I'll chase away
All too few who come to pray,
And I might even turn from You
As if You knew.

O Lord, just take it and let me see,
You rescue me.

I'm here, curled up from life on the floor–
Here, where I can't bear any more:
Where anger wears like torn up clothes–
It clearly shows.

O Lord, just take it and let me see,
You rescue me.

I know what David cried, I do–
I even cried the whole night through.
Grant me Your Spirit with Your grace,
To see Your face.

O Lord, just take it and let me see,
You rescue me–

My hope is in You.

No Shelter from the Pain

I wrote this poem after a woman's husband died of a massive heart attack. He died in my arms. Silence was the only expression of love I could offer at the time.

The last time I saw him
I was looking in his eyes.
I couldn't bring him back
And I couldn't tell you lies.
I watched you shifting worlds
From the pain that filled inside:

How hard it is
When there's no shelter from the pain.

I wish that God's Very Word
Would be all I need to say,
And I wish His Holy Spirit
Would do magic when I pray.
And I wish that His grace
Would drive the pain away:

How hard it is
When there's no shelter from the pain.

Oh, that I could take you
Along ten years from today,
Where the hardest of sorrow
Is a part of yesterday.
Yet although the days go by
I know pain is here to stay:

How hard it is
When there's no shelter from the pain.

There's no shelter from the pain,
And there's nothing I can say–
The only way out is
Through the pain.

The Cry of Job

I believe that Job was deeply hurt by the "friends" who came to help him because Job wasn't looking for advice. He knew the answers had to come from God himself. There is a lot for us to learn through Job's story.

My name is Job,
Not a man you should meet!
I once had it all and my life was so sweet.
I walked in His ways. I lived in His peace.
Nothing in this world challenged my belief.

Then.....
From nowhere came fire – some were caught in the heat.
From nowhere, wind – leaving blood on the street.
From nowhere, hate – some were lost in their sleep.
From nowhere, sores – from my head to my feet.

When.....
My friends stopped by, at first they did weep.
They stayed, we talked– for nights we did meet.
When finally they spoke to show me my need
My anguish outweighed the sands of the sea.

They said…..
I complained that God did not speak,
Since I had no visions or dreams in my sleep:
Pain was the teacher chastening me–
If my sin is confessed then He'd set me free.

With nothing left to say, fear was in their eyes–
Since all of this had come totally by surprise.

Come and sit with me,

Come and wait with me,

Until He lifts me up from my suffering.

Thoughts of Me Go, Too

As I followed the story of a young boy whose cancer was brought into remission, I found myself deeply moved by the dedicated nurses who cared for him. I tried to write this poem from the perspective of one of the nurses who cared for him.

Our First Meeting:

> The first night I saw you, I thought,
> One more heartache I can't take:
> No more energy to care;
> Not sure I could even try.
> Why did the Lord bring us together
> At this time?
>
> What drew me to your room that night?
> Your crying drew me there.
> (Not the one you wanted)
> I came in anyway.
> I stroked your hairless head and knew
> I had to stay.

Then You Went Home:

It was good to see your empty bed.
(We talked, we cried, we laughed
Before you left this place.)
But I came back to your room
And I prayed –
"Lord save him from the memories
Even if his thoughts of me go, too!
And fill the gap that relates to me –
Fill it with eternity in You."

Years Later:

Once I stopped by
Just to see you playing.
Someone said, "Who's waving?"
You said you didn't know.
You waved back to me
And I went on my way-
For you are to relive not one
Past painful day-
But that's okay, I guess.

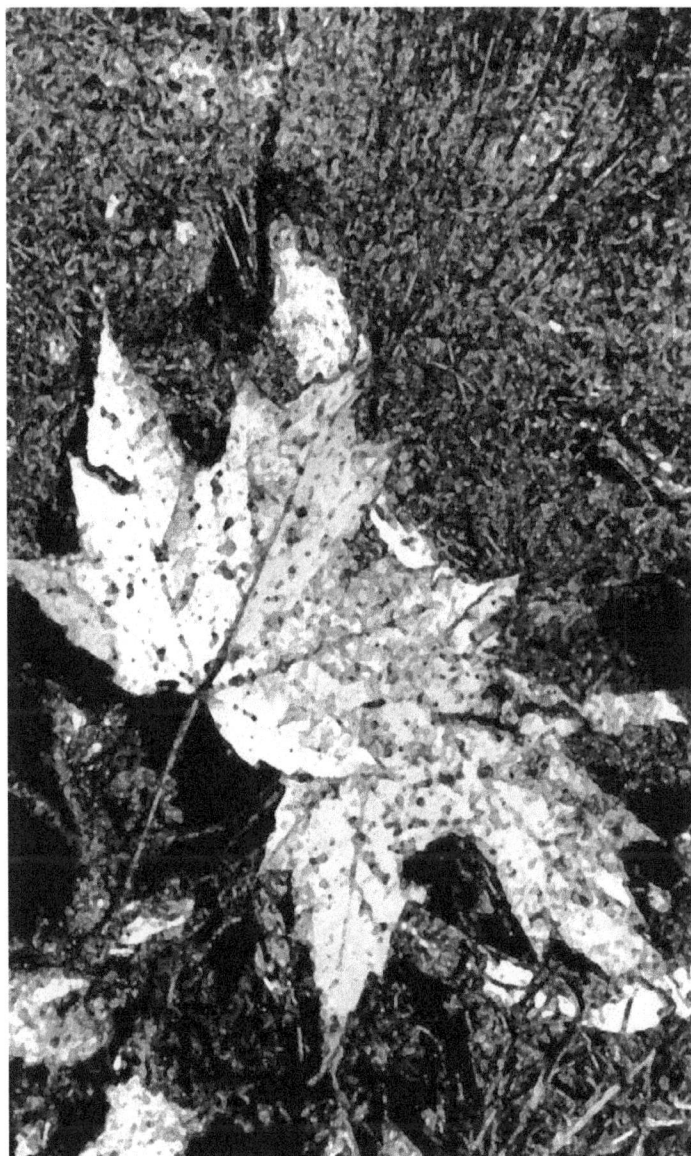

Let Go of Your Hold

I woke up crying,
"Let go of your hold!"
From a recurring dream,
Where I'm holding on to you,
Pulling you back to me,
And you're holding on to something–
Something I can't see.

I know your anger's not with me–
It's a lie that you've been told.
What else can I do
To save us two?
Let go of your hold!

By the power of the Spirit,
On the promise of the Lord,
Let go of your hold!

I guess it's in His hands;
I have to let it be.
If I press too hard you'll shatter.
The means don't really matter.
His love knows best.

His timing is key.
Let go of your hold.

You must stop lying-
No more defying.
Inside I'm crying,
While you're denying.
By the power of the Spirit,
On the promise of the Lord,
Let go of your hold!

Time to Heal

How do we counteract the hurts that build over time in relationships? Miscommunication leads to misunderstanding until it becomes seemingly impossible to openly talk and resolve the differences. In some cases, with some relationships, we may never find peace until we enter into Christ's presence.

I approached you eagerly at first
With **healed-over wounds**.
All relationships bear the marks,
I was not naïve.
Small scratches, at first insignificant,
And I healed fast.

But **wounded again and again**,
The wounds spread.
Instigating, propagating
As I approached you again and again.
There was no time to heal
Between hurts.

The **open wounds** made me think ahead,
Made my approach slower

And slower until
You sensed it.
You saw it as distance between us
And it became
Almost impossible to go back, start over,
Start afresh.

How can time heal
When the need for healing is so immediate?

Maybe we'll just pass on into eternity
With our wounds still raw and stinging.

Listening Needs

This poem was written about a woman whose parents were very dysfunctional in their relationship with her. She never had a childhood. She never had someone to truly listen to her, although she emptied herself by listening to others.

To Myself:

> When I close my eyes
> I see a little girl.
> Why can't she speak?
> Is no one listening to her?
> She's serving the tea
> To someone else–
> Always to someone else.
>
> What if her needs
> Are too great?
> Who will dry her tears?
> Who will hold her close?
> Who will tame her fears?
> She's more like a mother
> Than she needs to be,

And far too young
To play that role.

To the Lord:

Lord, I come to Your Word.
Day and night
I come to Your Word.
When others drain my cup
Who will fill me up
By listening–
Listening to me?
Who's listening–
Listening to me?

To Myself:

When I open my eyes
I look in the mirror.
"Why can't she speak?
Is no one listening to her?"
She's still serving the tea
To someone else-
Always to someone else.

To the Lord:

> How do I make my burdens light
> So I can carry someone else's?
> What if I'm lost in the night,
> How can I show someone the day?
> Where will my strength come from?
> Where will my hope come from?

To Myself:

> I'm more like a child
> Than I need to be,
> And far too old
> To play that role:
> I have a whole life of listening needs.

Deep Deep Water

How many of us become immobilized by the fear that an unbearable release of deep-seated issues (such as guilt, shame, neglect, and abuse) could come rushing out uncontrollably if we allow ourselves to open up to God's grace and love? This fear builds like deep, deep water behind a dam that needs to break.

Someone like You said,
"Follow me"
So I took one step forward
And fell back three.
Going up or down?
I couldn't see.

I heard someone say,
"Try again"
Come in from the cold,
Shelter from the rain.
But I gave up hoping
I would ever change.

I'm stuck in the shadow
Of a great big dam;
And there's cold, cold water

Behind that dam.

Deep, deep water behind the dam.
Deep, deep water keeps me where I am.
Deep, deep water behind the dam.

When no one was looking
I raised my hand,
So that someone like You
Could help me stand.

When no one was looking
I raised my hand:
"Don't leave me here!"

Baptize me,
Set me free.
Let the dam break,
Let it dissipate,
Let it wash over me.

I'm stuck in quicksand,
Standing at the base
Of a great big dam
And You said,

"Follow me."

Love was Wanting More

Solitude arises in a falling snow–

I stepped out and it seemed the cold
Was the price I'd have to pay
Just to have some time alone.

Solitude arises in a falling snow–

I walked until the houses behind me
Fused into the gray;
Until the world was lost in a storm;
Until I felt more alone than I ever had before–
And in all that was wanting, love was wanting more.
(Love was not enough to bring about love.)

Solitude arises in a falling snow–

And once again, all alone,
On a rock deep in the woods
Where the snow fell in silence,
There I had a place to go
To find what I had found before:
In all that was wanting, love was wanting more.

Not Why? But Who?

When you find yourself struggling with the questions "Why?" and "What if?" try a different question, simply ask "Who?" Who controls the universe? Who is Lord and King over all creation? Who sent His son to redeem His people?

My Questioning:

> Why did it rain today?
> Why did my plans get changed?
> Why did her newborn die?
> Why did their dad say, "Bye?"
> What makes the nations war?
> What is a drought good for?
> Where will the lightening strike?
> What should the world be like?

The Lord Replies:

> Listen now and I will speak.
> I will question you,
> You shall answer Me.
>
> Who made the birds to fly?
> Who made the stars and sky?

Who knew you from the womb?
Who raised Christ from the tomb?
Who opened heaven's gate?
Who gives you hope to wait?
Whose knowledge will transcend?
Whose kingdom never ends?

My Prayer:

Raise me up knowing Who
Rules with justice and grace.
Raise me up seeing You
At the end of the race.
Raise me up from the dust.
Raise me up in Your name.
Raise me up in the promise
That You're coming again.

I've been looking for answers,
Searching for clues-
You've brought me back to the question,
It's not "Why?" it's "Who?"

Whose Father are You?

Ever since I can remember
My father's arms were always empty–
Not of someone else, just of me.

Ever since I can remember
My father's few encouraging words
Were meant for someone else, not for me.

Since I never had a father
To seek me out because he loves me,
Unconditionally – just for me:

Since I never loved a father
And I draw back when You come towards me,
Who will bridge the gap, You to me?

If You call Yourself my Father,
Do You think that You can take
All the anger I'll create?

If You call Yourself my Father,
Are You ready to bear
Every unleashed tear?

If You call Yourself my Father,
Can You take a solemn vow?
Cause I'll die if You leave me– *don't leave me now!*

> **Father**, seek me face to face–
> I've no strength left; there's no safe place,
> Just an empty void here in me.

> **Father**, take me by the heart–
> I think that's where redemption starts.
> Say you'll love someone just like me?

I've been scarred by a father in the flesh;
I desire his love nonetheless.
Can a Father in the Spirit pass the test?

> **Whose Father are You, anyway?**

Lighter Side of Life

It's not easy to help someone who chooses to make the same mistakes over and over again. Few of us can sustain such compassion without burning out. This is why the power to love must come from the Spirit of God!

Just yesterday
I walked with a friend
I hadn't seen in a while,
Since he had lost his smile.

He was homeless again
And I couldn't take him in
For the stench of his breath
And the marks on his skin.

So I found him
A run-down place to stay,
And I passed on some cash
With some food instead of trash.

But then I went away.
I had to get away.
Despite the tender mercies
His desire is to stray.

(Lord,
Take me to the lighter side of life for a while.
I'm exhausted, spent, worn out-
No more love to be turned out.
Take me to the lighter side of life.)

It's not his past,
Nor what he brings today,
Nor the hard road ahead
That pushes me away.

And it's not his felt needs
That really turn me off.
What really does me in
Is his arrogant face of sin!

(Lord,
Lay me down in green pastures,
Lead me beside the still waters,
And take me to the lighter side of life for a while.
Take me to the lighter side of life.)

Redeeming Love

Tell me I'm dreaming.
This can't be real.
This can't be real.
This can't be real!

I saw that look on your face.
I felt your heart about to break.
I saw hope slip away–
Tomorrow lost today.

One more thing in life gone wrong
Doesn't make you who you are.
See what the Lord will do;
Greater love He has for you.

I'll catch your tears as they fall.
I'll stay forever at your side,
Until there comes the time
Eternal love refines.

But as fear builds inside
Don't mistake this love of mine

For what the Lord *will do*.
Greater love He has for you!

> Though it's *my* love that you'll see,
> Though it's *my* love that you'll feel,
> I'm just a shadow of the Lord's
> **Redeeming love.**

> The redeeming love of Christ
> Is *your* power for life–
> **Redeeming love.**

> By grace defined,
> By love refined–
> **Redeeming love.**

Someone with Skin On

When times are tough it helps to physically touch someone or feel someone's presence beside us. This is not to say that God's love is insufficient, but just to say that we are human. God gave us each other for this very reason. 2 Corinthians 1:3-7 explains that God provides for us through each other.

> The storm raged outside.
> Lightening hit a nearby tree.
> I ran to my mom,
> And stood beside her bed.
> She said,
> "**God is in control**.
> Your fears, He knows.
> Though you may not feel it,
> He holds you close."
> I said, "*I need someone with skin on!*"
>
> The storm raged inside-
> Tragedy of the heart.
> I found myself alone.
> I stood at your door.
> You said,
> "**God is in control**.

Your fears, He knows.
Though you may not feel it,
He holds you close."
I said, "*I need someone with skin on!*"

      (Lord,
      I know you're always there-
      But it sure helps
      To have someone to touch,
      Someone to see,
      Someone who speaks
      And holds onto me.)

A phone call can lift me when I'm down.
A card in the mail I can read,
When I need,
If I keep it around.
But there's nothing like the healing touch
Of someone who cares-
Someone with skin on.

Isn't it True

It's a painful reality that God humbles us most and teaches us best amid the struggles of life. I wish it were not true. But I also know that I could never go back to way I used to be before I experienced all my struggles and pain. God changed me, matured me, loved me, and showed me His grace. These gifts are priceless!!

After *all* I've been through………..

Isn't it true,
One thing I'll never do is go back to the way I used to be:
Mind over reality;
Afloat on a blissful sea;
Lacking true sincerity.

Lord, lift me from the pit but keep me near the edge.
Clear the sky away but keep the rain a threat.
I've been changed, in *Your* name, I'm not the same.
By Your name I've been changed.

(If I had the choice
Would I still walk down the road You put me on?
If I had the choice
Would I still go through what You ordained me to?

When is the cost too high to gain from earthly loss
And change a sinful heart?)

After *all* I've been through...........

Isn't it true,
I had to stop resisting, fall before You, start admitting
So You could start redeeming, grace come streaming,
Raise me in Him.

I'm changed forever and for the better,
And my broken heart sings.

When a broken heart sings, it sings of joy.
When a broken heart sings, it sings with hope.

Lord, keep me near the edge
where my broken heart sings!

One Child Too Many

A child with one arm-
The other gone
And yet he still walks amid the mines.

A child with no family, no home.
She was sold
For being a girl- wrong place, wrong time.

A child laid to rest
When a driver's test
Failed to protect her from a DUI.

> From the TV to the news,
> From the street into the home,
> Everywhere I turn, everywhere I go,
> Children are hurting-
> **One child too many**.

A child gives up the fight,
Cries all night
With no strength left to search for food.

A child runs loose
From constant abuse,
With no one to say, "Come home soon."

A child who'll never know
His name, his home,
His mother's voice outside the womb.

From China to Africa,
From India to Pan Am-
All across the world, here in my home town,
Children are hurting-
One child too many.

It wasn't meant to be this way.
The children were to be blessed
And set aside from all the rest
For special hugs,
Special kisses,
Special love.

A curl on the top of her head
That bounces as she runs.
The bluest of eyes,
An innocent smile,
That warms my heart.
This is the way it was meant to be.

So I hold back the tears-
(If I let *one* fall, a thousand will follow)
Until He comes again.

Lord,
Yours is the day when the children will be free-
Oh come that day, *soon*!

Until that day, I'll hold back the tears-
Yet with the hope that You hold dear

Not one child

But many!

Call on Me

Honesty in relationships causes tension. We want to be honest with each other, yet there are things we shouldn't say without much forethought and prayer. It can be hard to hold things in but it can be even harder to fix relationships after we've said things we shouldn't have said in the way we said them. I believe that Jesus is our pressure relief valve– telling us to "Call on Me". He is the master of relationships and the guide to our hearts.

Last night I couldn't sleep
So I got up from my bed.
My nerves in hyper speed,
Too much stuff was in my head.
Some things I just can't say:
Words can heal and words can break.
If I keep them in I'll burst.
I don't want to make mistakes.
Who can I call?

There seems to be a limit
To being more than friends.
Don't want to push that limit
As limits have their ends.
Can I hold Him to His Word,
And give it all to Him?

When I need to get it out
And I just can't keep it in,
Who can I call?

We stand closer than we like to think
In being torn apart.
Being silent is a driver,
And in silence it could start.

Love means holding back sometimes
Knowing it could cause a fall,
But holding back can hurt a lot
So I need someone to call.
Who can I call?

Call on Me, He says,
When you're weak and heavy laden.

Call on Me, He says,
Place those burdens in My care.

I am
The one
Who has numbered every hair.

So call on Me, He says,
There's nothing else to do but
Call on Me.

I'll take You at *Your* Word.
I'll see what *You* will do
With the things beyond my grasp-
I'll call on You.

Way Out

When we pursue people we care about, we allow the Lord to use us as His human shepherd's staff to retrieve His sheep, to give them a safe Way Out of their troubles. I have tried to capture, in this work, the words that we might communicate to people we love who are sinking quickly in the ocean of despair and suffering.

When your world has crumbled down,
And there's no hope at all around;

When you're tempted beyond
What you can bear,
I'll be there.
If I'm not inside when it all begins,
You'll have to let me in-
So let me in.

Pick up the phone.
Reach out and grab the phone,
Don't let it ring.
Although I'm not the one
Who can change your life
(That angel of relief

Who doesn't seem to come
To get you out).

Open the door.
Get the door when I knock,
For He's a faithful God
And He won't let you walk
Where all hope is at risk.
For when you come across
Much more than you can bear
There's a way out.

Answer the phone.
Open the door.
It's from the Lord:
Way out!

Healthy Life Press

Books, eBooks, DVDs

Arvada, Colorado

A Small, Independent Christian Publisher
with a big mission—to help people live
healthier lives physically, emotionally,
spiritually, and relationally.

For a downloadable PDF catalog of our resources,
and access to free sample excerpts from our books,
visit: *www.healthylifepress.com*

1-877-331-2766 | *info@healthylifepress.com*

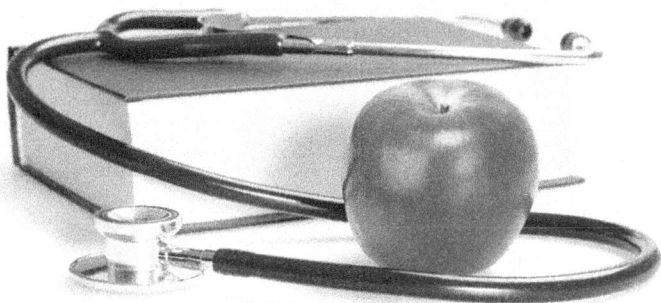

www.ingramcontent.com/pod-product-compliance
Lightning Source LLC
Chambersburg PA
CBHW060121050426
42448CB00010B/1975